Once
upon
a time
I was...

BIS Publishers
Building Het Sieraad
Postjesweg 1
1057 DT Amsterdam
The Netherlands
T +31 (0)20 515 02 30
bis@bispublishers.nl
www.bispublishers.nl

www.onceuponatimeiwas.com
www.facebook.com/onceuponatimeiwasbook

Design: Lennart Veenendaal - www.idvisual.nl

ISBN 978 90 6369 346 6
Second printing 2014

Copyright © 2014 Lavinia Bakker and BIS Publishers.

About the 'author'

Have you ever wondered about your grandfather's favourite song or about your grandmother's hopes and dreams? I have and this is how I came up with the idea for this book. My name is Lavinia Bakker. I never knew my grandfather. I would have liked to know so much more about him than the few stories my parents told me. Surely, you have a person in your life whose memory (even if it's your own) you wish to treasure. This book offers space to record beliefs and life lessons, to be cherished forever.

If you don't feel the need to give this journal to someone special, how about bringing it along on a holiday with friends or fill it in yourself! The answers and conversations that this book will spark will brighten your life.

Instructions

I've left plenty of room to personalize the book to your liking. For example, you can scribble down a thought, add more text to an answer, draw something, or put pictures in.

X **Always write too much.**

X **Always tell the truth.**

X **Add 'because' to your own liking.**

X **Don't try to write it all down at once.**

X **Include all of your life's best experiences.**

X **Use a big black marker to cross out the questions you don't want to answer.**

X **Add dates to the answers that can change over time.**

X **Be colourful! Write in different colours to add even more of a personal touch.**

. . . .

gave me
this book

date:

The
chapters
of my life

General
info

My name is

My date of birth is

My place of birth is

My parents are/were

My siblings are/were

My grandparents are/were

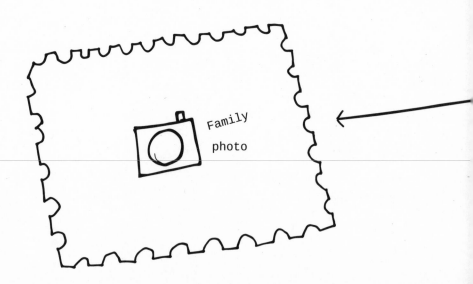

Family photo

This is
my family
tree

I am

in a
relationship

single

engaged

ph oto

divorced

married

I have/don't have kids, and their names are

My name was chosen because

If I was of the other sex, my name would have been

My first memory is

My favourite memory of growing up is

little
me

My worst memory of growing up is

Growing up, my parents were

◯ loving   ◯ caring

◯ consistent

◯ strict

◯ open   ◯ easy

◯ other:

The relationship with my parents was

I had the best relationship with my mom/dad

My favourite memory of my parents is

My parents taught me from a young age that

The relationship with my siblings was

I had the best relationship with my

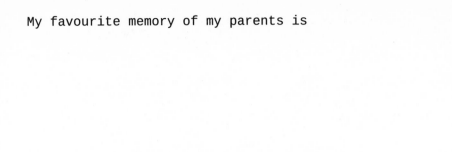

17

My favourite memory of my siblings is

My grandparents were   growing up

The relationship with my grandparents was

I had the best relationship with my grandmother/grandfather

My favourite memory of my grandparents is

Our family can best be described as

19

I believed in Santa Claus until I was

and   told me that he doesn't exist

Holidays such as Christmas/Thanksgiving/Easter were spent

Birthdays were spent

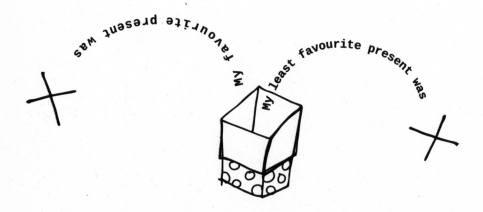

My favourite present was

My least favourite present was

20

I look most like : ....

Games we played were

Television shows we watched were

`I was a`

◯ sweet   ◯ strong-minded

        ◯ shy

                ◯ active

    ◯ easy

                    `kid`

As a child, I was (or so other people tell me)

As a child, I had the following diseases

The most mischievous thing I did was

I got punished when

I grew up in

The house we lived in

looked like this

My bedroom looked like this

The posters on my wall were from

25

My favourite cuddly toy was

My favourite children's book was

My favourite games were

My favourite toy was

My favourite TV show was

if

my life were a song, it would be

Some had we pets of pictures

We had pets   **yes / no**

they were

I really looked up to

Important people in my childhood were

Lessons I learned were

I was afraid of

I played the following sports

This was my first good friend. This was my first good friend. This was my first good friend. This was my first good friend. This was my first good friend.

name:

I am still in contact with him/her - yes / no

More of my school friends were

Kindergarten was

Primary school was

I liked/didn't like to go to school because

My favourite thing to do in school was

33

My least favourite thing to do in school was

My favourite after-school activities were

I bullied/got bullied

My favourite teachers were

When I was young, I wanted to be

Good
times
...

Some of my

favourite

pictures

These are the
technological
developments I
witnessed

Major events

that made a
big impression
on me

High school
& Work

The high school I went to was named

When I look back at high school, I think of

Me during
**high
school**

The best
cheating
advice I have is

My favourite subjects were

The subject I was best at was

The subject I wasn't very good at

My best grade was

The diplomas and/or certificates I obtained are

I was a popular kid

yes   **no**

My idols were

I moved out of my parents' house when I was

My father worked as

Do you **recognize me?**

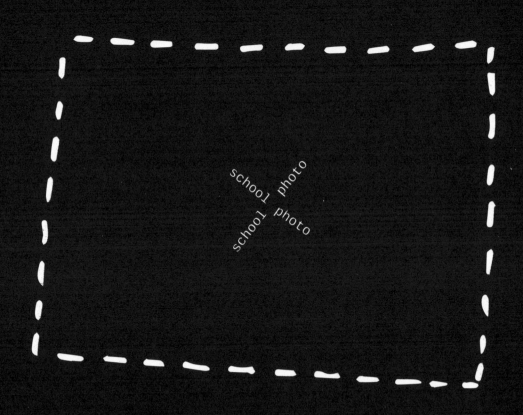

school photo school photo school photo school photo

My mother worked as

My first job was

My jobs during high school were

The first thing I bought with my own money was

if

I could witness a
major event in
the past, present
or future, it
would be:

My favourite job was

The job I've had the longest was as

I loved

My favourite thing to do on a day off

I did/did not get the job I always wanted because

The best business advice I have is

Find a treasure

I have hidden something for you to find. This map will show you where it is

Happi
ness
&
Heart
ache

My first date was with

and we went to

My first kiss was at the age of   with

and I thought it was

My first time was at the age of   with

and I thought it was

What I find most attractive in a woman/man is

My favourite memory when it comes to love is

My worst memory when it comes to love is

The most romantic thing I've ever done is

The most romantic thing I've ever experienced was

A perfect date for me is

My best advice on love is

The best flirting advice I have is

My advice
when it comes to

heartache

My first great love was

My first relationship was with

The flames who broke my heart are

This is the love of my life T

The love of my life is

I met him/her at

is the love of my life

What I find most attractive in my significant other is

I got proposed to by

I proposed to

We got married on   . . . .

Our wedding day was ♡

Some pictures of my kid(s)

* **We have** .... **kid(s)**

I experienced the birth of my kid(s) as

What I think is the best thing about having kids

The relationship with my kids can be described as

My favourite memories with my kids are

The relationship I have/had with my parents can be
described as

My parents taught me that

The relationship I now have with my siblings can be
described as

if

I could possess a superpower I would want it to be:

This is

my best

friend

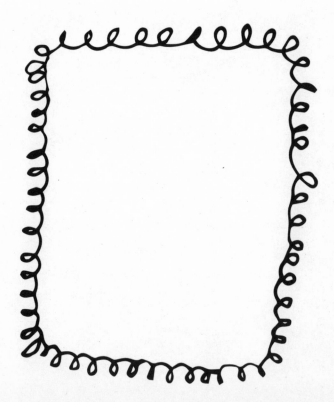

The most fun thing to do with my friends is

The most important qualities in a friend are

My greatest hits

1

2

3

4

5

6

7

8

9

10

e most This is

This is

This is music st. styl

music

that I

love the mos

♪

I left a copy
with this book

These are **tickets and pictures**
of the best concert(s)
I've ever been to

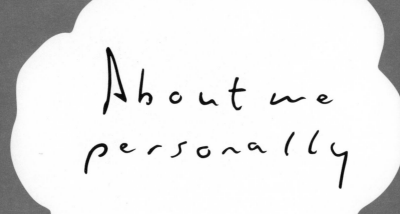

About me
personally

My best qualities are

My worst qualities are

...was the most fun I ever had

The thing I find ugliest about myself is

The thing I find most beautiful about myself is

My favourite thing to do is

My least favourite thing to do is

I am good at

I am not good at

I am most proud of

I am least proud of

The 3 most important things

in my life are

The worst thing I've ever experienced was

The hardest decision I've ever had to make was

if

I could be born again, I would prefer to be:

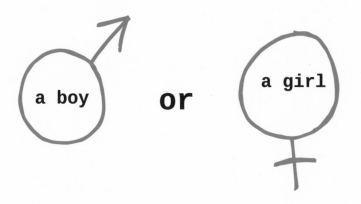

a boy   or   a girl

because:

I deal with setbacks by

In times of sorrow this thought gives me strength

My best advice is

My perfect day looks like

Places
I have been

My
favourite
holiday
memories

This place in the world
is a must-see

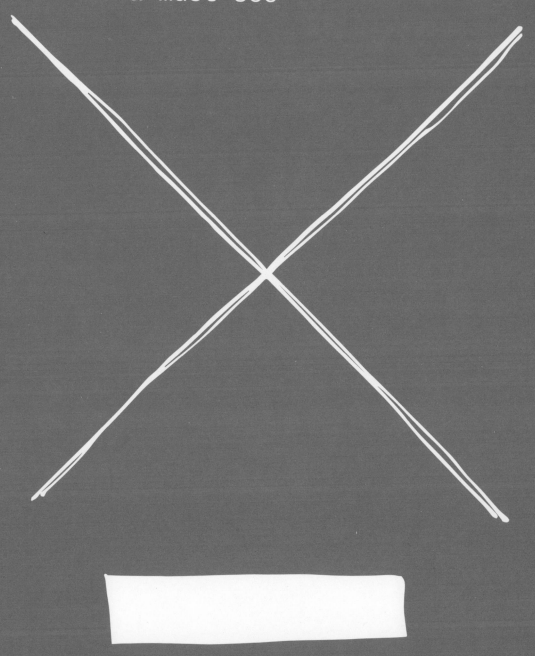

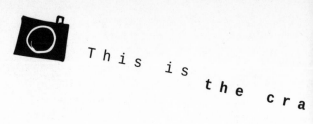

This is the cra

I am most grateful for

The best compliment I've ever been given was

This is what makes me tick

.

The thing I can't stand is

t f a c e I c a n m a k e

You can wake me up for

Happiness to me is

if

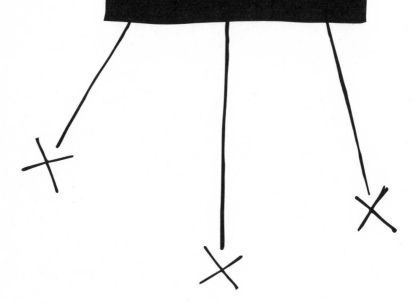

I could invite
3 people (dead
or alive) for
dinner, they
would be:

because:

I
regret
not doing this :

Highlights in my life were

The best advice I've ever received was

The worst advice I've ever received was

A turning point in my life was when

94 This is the shape of my hand

The worst thing I've ever done is

Things I am most sorry about are

The biggest lie I've ever told was

My deepest secret is

The most embarrassing thing I've ever experienced was

If there was something I could do differently, it would be

This is a
self-portrait

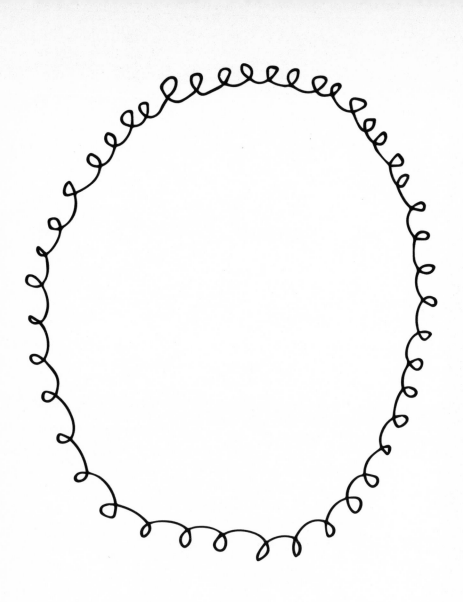

was my biggest inspiration

98

taught me the most in my life

changed me the most in my life

I owe a lot to

My dreams came true

yes   **no**

I still want to learn how to

If I could change anything in the world it would be

If there would be a story about my life, it would be called

If I could be compared to a character from a film or a TV show, it would be

I believe in

I don't believe in

I think that when we die we go to

People also call me

My nickname is

I voted for

because

My hobbies are

My quirk is

I experimented with drugs

yes   **no**

My best cleaning advice is

My 3 most valuable material possessions are

if

I could
change my
first name,
I would
change it
to:

This place is where I
spent most of my time
writing in this book

quiz

You can find the answers
in the back of this book
on page:

----

ques-
tion   ①

multiple   **a**
choice
answer   **b**

           c

           ②

           a

           b

           c

③

a
b
c

④

a
b
c

⑤

a
b
c

⑥

a
b
c

⑦

open
answer

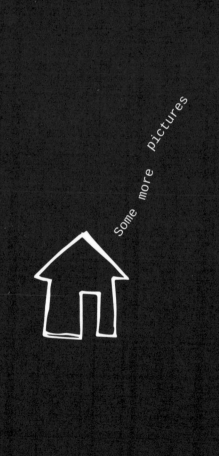

Some more pictures

All the
addresses
I have
called home

favou
rites

Favourite memory

Favourite 3 movies

Favourite writer

Favourite 3 TV shows

Favourite 3 books

Favourite play

Favourite saying

Favourite

Poem

I love:

summer

spring

autumn

winter

because:

114

Favourite one-liner

Favourite 3 brands

Favourite holiday destination

Favourite hotel

pasted here

This is my favourite flower

115

if

I could stay a certain age forever, I would choose to stay:

Favourite city

Favourite foreign city

Favourite country

Favourite restaurant

Favourite cocktail

Favourite drink

Favourite meal

Least favourite meal

yum yum

yum

yum

yum

Best recipe

yum

Favourite snack

Favourite ice cream

Favourite fruit/vegetable

Favourite pet(s)

This is my
favourite sweet

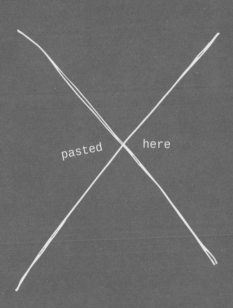

pasted   here

My favourite perfume/aftershave smells like this... spray away! My

I left a
sample
with this
book

name:

122

Favourite animal

Favourite car

Favourite song

Favourite singer

123

I got stranded on a deserted island, these are the 3 things I could not live without:

Favourite music genre

Favourite music album

Favourite colour

Favourite house I lived in

Favourite game

Favourite sport

Favourite sports moment

Favourite sportsman/woman

Most beautiful man/woman

if

I could
relive a day
of my life,
it would be:

And
some more
pictures

I would
like to
say this
to...

Contra
dictions

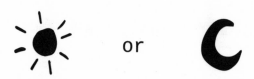

or

private   or   public

scared   or   brave

high   or   low

or

simple   or   complicated

neat   or   sloppy

fate   or   coincidence

save   or   spend

■   or   ☐

sweet   or   salty

dog   or   cat

above   or   beneath

✚   or   ▬

together   or   alone

going out   or   staying in

even   or   uneven

lazy   or   energetic

modern   or   old-fashioned

city   or   countryside

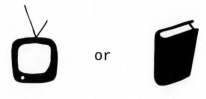   or

optimistic   or   pessimistic

listen   or   see

future   or   past

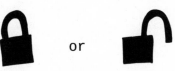   or

games to win   or   games for fun

if

I had a
time machine
I would
travel to:

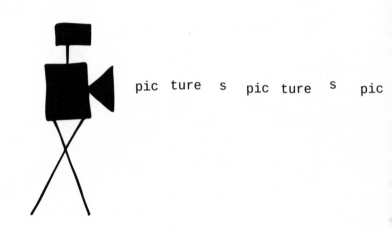

pic ture s pic ture s pic

s   pic ture   s   pic ture s pic

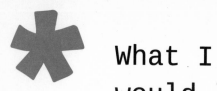

What I would like to add

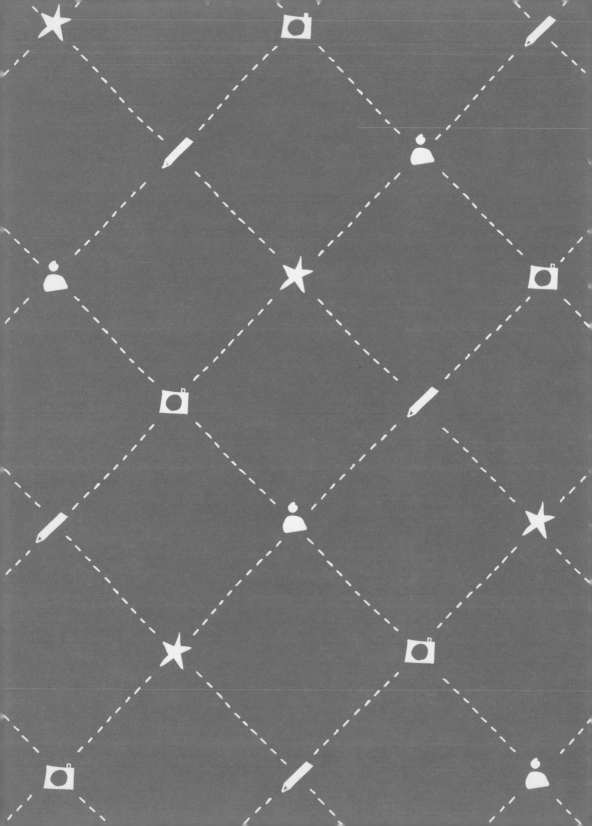